Dance Caprice

by Christopher Bunting

for Cello and Piano

Oxford University Press

DANCE - CAPRICE

CHRISTOPHER BUNTING

Printed in Great Britain
OXFORD UNIVERSITY PRESS, MUSIC DEPARTMENT, GREAT CLARENDON STREET, OXFORD OX2 6DP

CELLO

For D.L.

DANCE - CAPRICE

CHRISTOPHER BUNTING

Allegro, energico

Grazioso e pochissimo meno mosso

poco a poco al tempo primo

Notes for Cellist
1. Play bar 1, and similar figures, at the heel.
2. Play bar 7, and similar, detaché, in the middle of the bow.
3. Play 14 from left to right, [also bars 82-5]
4. Play bars 22-26 at the heel.
5. Play 55-6 at the heel, slightly nearer the fingerboard than usual.

Dance - Caprice

4

Dance - Caprice

Dance - Caprice

Processed and printed by
Halstan & Co. Ltd., Amersham, Bucks., England

OXFORD UNIVERSITY PRESS

ISBN 978-0-19-355750-5